33

poetry
by
christina deming

PublishAmerica
Baltimore

© 2007 by Christina Deming.
All rights reserved. No part of this book may be reproduced, stored in a retrieval system or transmitted in any form or by any means without the prior written permission of the publishers, except by a reviewer who may quote brief passages in a review to be printed in a newspaper, magazine or journal.

First printing

At the specific preference of the author, PublishAmerica allowed this work to remain exactly as the author intended, verbatim, without editorial input.

ISBN: 1-4241-7325-6
PUBLISHED BY PUBLISHAMERICA, LLLP
www.publishamerica.com
Baltimore

Printed in the United States of America

dedicated

to

those who
didn't let me give up
on a dream—
family, friends, and
most of all,
Lord Jesus Christ

Shirley,

Friend, mentor, sister in Christ – you are a blessing in my life.
May God bless you!

Christina Deming
PHIL. 4:13

contents

observations

the storm inside 11
jagged lane 12
more than myself 13
looking back 14
sweet peas 15
beautiful 18
whispers 19
dust to dust 20
true happiness 23
see the trees 24
connected 25
the blues 27
2-3-4 is the actual date today 28
in October with you 29
little bug 31
deep blue night 33
garden in a sandbox 34

love

among the ashes 39
every man craves 40
deep fire of love 41
A Father's Love 43
above the clouds 44

right out loud 45
thank you for your prayers 47
power of Your love 48
snowshoeing in flip-flops 50
Everything 51
loving 53
undeserving heir 55

faith

broken paradise 59
there is a reason 61
i can begin again 63
make it Yours 64
let me shine 65
from my knees 67
daughter of the King 68
mysteries too awesome 69
rejoice! 71
ultimate defense 72
bright inside 73
to my knees 74
He is in control 75
catch a fish or two 76
Peace in Your Grace 77
humble stature 78
worthy 79
hope 80
Lord, open their hearts 81
a prayer for the new year 83
in God's hands 84
until it overflows 85
Jesus on my side 87

33

observations

the storm inside

i stand now
  on the foundation of my soul
  where what you love,
    what you believe,
    where you belong
      and what you know
become
  one
    the wings of God's kisses
  butterflies on your heart
    the peace of grace
  constant comfort
    in a chaotic race
of conformity,
      money
    and might
      a little out of sight
of the old me
      but still
          revealed by His love
eyes open
    arms raised to eternity above
i thank
  and pray
      and brave the storm inside

jagged lane

I cannot overcome it
  as I continue
    to watch myself become it
and am overwhelmed
  by the simultaneous
vastness
     and nothingness
      of the world
still a little girl
      feeling old
scared
    I stare up
      the jagged lane
with dreams of
    peace
      echoing in the back
of my brain
     and beckoning
    me to escape

more than myself

the tick-tock
    I said would never come
    rings louder in my heart
while I still struggle to part
      with selfishness
        sluggishness
           fatigue
    out of my league
    and yet yearning
      for more
a meaning
      above money
    or accomplishment
    a commitment
to more than
    myself or this world

looking back

I wonder now,
  as Ms. Denny did,
    where does the time go?

I don't know
      what happens to
      the minutes
    that makes them disappear—

do they run and hide
      among the warm shadows
of sunny summer
afternoons?

Do they swim like loons,
    diving out of our sight
    into the pools
      of our tears?

Do the years skip happily
    away across the
        snow-covered hills
and live there in silence
    with our fears?

I can hear the hope
      of yesterday
    in the tired rhythm
      of my heart
whispering in my ear again
    on the eve
        of another new start

sweet peas

i've stumbled onto peace before
waiting quietly at the door
of my confused heart
i've snatched it up
used it up
only to cry for more

when peace is gone
I blame the world
the man
the day
I find no comfort in what people say
their frantic voices of help
I push away

my self strength is good enough
but, where's the peace?
Where's the love?
In dreams that pass with the light,
in the stars, the blanket of night?
Surely not in my fear
that spawns the pain
that leads to tears
of memories
free
to fly
toward peace
to cry
for each
broken soul
that enters in
to my own
for just one moment

time spent
imprisoned
by the vision
without the means
or support
or help

help!
Can I find it hear
it in your promises
on the petals
of the roses
in your heart?
Will I find it hear
it inside
my own mind
before time
tears this world
and me
apart?

No.
no peace finds me
til I find it
through God
through love
through the self

i've abandoned
for the rush
the race of
everyday denial
of what's real
of what I feel
instead of what

I know
peace will bring
me nothing
until I give
my self
to peace,
to love

until I can believe
i'll stumble on
to peace
only now and then
finding only false
equanimity
in the eyes
of friends

until I can
until I do
until
until…
when?

Ah, sweet peace
come in,
sit down

stay.

beautiful

only God knows
    true beauty
  only He can define
      the sublime
for see how we
    change our minds
  with the times
as to what
    is beautiful?

whispers

even when
   I think all
I can hear
    is the chaos
in my own mind

God gently whispers
   in my ear
and fear
      flies away

dust to dust

visions and letters
spinning round in my senses
curving into words about
love, death and climbed fences
line after line
they fall, ink to paper—
originally mine
is secrecy safer?

To keep these truths and rhymes
to myself
I have many times
in the past, on a shelf
deep in the hidden core
of my heart or my being
but silence no more—
I must say what I'm seeing

I look to the world
from the hitchin' post of this town
through the eyes of one girl
trying not to get down
thinking of famine and drought
in far away places
wanting to get out—

escape from the lonely, tired faces
of men who have killed their spirit
working til their whole self aches
glory—needing to get near it
wondering what it takes

just as the women's' dreams
quiver at the hope of
conquering hardship til it seems
there's time for nothing but love

Feeling close beside me
I find children aspiring to be
just like the men and women I see
never knowing
the truth about heroes
just growing
but, then, how could they know
that mortals stay in their tiny shell
too quickly take leave and are gone
so many of my gods have fessed up and fell
and yet as they do, so I must go on
watching and listening to
the world going by
attempting to pray as good Christians do
only once every night stopping to cry.
And still the words rumble,
they turn
and they tumble
burn-
-ing their way to a page or a mat-
-ted shape
to be stared at

people, you gape
as do i
but do we comprehend
and why
when life ends
do we weep
while all through its course

we keep
suffering pain or remorse
sobbing and coping

and me,
I keep hoping
to be
a help to this world
that I'm living in
one wide-eyed girl
watching the sin
and the healing
as people go,

feeling
until they know
wherever they travel
life will unravel
rumbling and turning
tumbling and burning
until ashes remain
and we are lain
bodies in the ground
when our souls've finally found
what they must—
dust to dust.

true happiness

thank you, Lord
for these dishes to wash
for it means
we are well fed

thank you, Lord
for this bed to make,
we have somewhere
to rest our heads

thank you, Lord
for all the chores
that mean we
are so blessed—

for a home, our health
and each other to love—

for that is
true happiness.

see the trees

see the trees
   how they grow
upward
      and grow
year after year
   and don't know
when
     the axe
      or disease
           will come
      to them
    and end
       the simple
beauty of
      their
       silent
         life
you'll here no complaint
    from the trees,
 only feel the gentle
breeze their leaves
     yield to
view with awe
    their fall
     splendor
see the trees, and remember
  you are a branch
     in the tree of life

connected

my world is so small,
my Lord, my King
and yet sometimes
all the little things
that shape it
take the wind
right out of me

and all i can see
is my small world
bearing down
on all sides,
a monster created
by the sound
my fear makes,

and everything
in my little world
shakes
until i'm hiding
inside
my bandaged façade,
with no one to
turn to

but you, my God
see it all—
know all the intricacies
of my small world

and the number of
hairs on the head
of the girl
halfway around the globe
who feels
just like i do
and thinks she's alone
and it's all too much

until she meets You
and feels the everlasting touch
of the One who
made eternity,
and can see
the unseen,
heal her
and me,
and the whole world

she and i are blinded to
by the limits
of our earthly eyes
our little worlds
so far apart,
and yet
connected
by the thread
You sewed the skies
together with,
the living Bread
who gave His life
to keep us
from the pit

the blues

it's true
    misery loves company
the blues
    always make me
  feel better
the sad long screams
      and soft moans
giggles
    of horns
 subtle beat
   of the drums
 a drug that
  induces you
  to move
and the wails
    of the one
  with the voice
that mirrors
   the impressions on
  so many
      men's souls
the rhythm gets
    into your heart
floats away your pain
    on the strings of the bass
til you're lost in the sound
    and there's no trace
      of your blues

2-3-4
is the actual date today

the poems are coming now
like tears
the years still peel away
like fresh pear skin
from the child within
when i am scared
when i bare
my soul to you
when i look
for love
in your eyes
and i try
to glue
my smile back on

in October with you

the midnight fog
  that crawls into the dawn
 like magician's smoke,
slowly fades
  under golden rays
    as the sun breaks
the dam,
  flows over
 jumping fish,
   and fluffy flies
     tied to spider lines
  that stretch and float
across the wide,
   ripping roar of the water
the river
 tugs at your legs
as it rushes past
    you feel the "thump!"
 you jerk your rod—it bends
you reel
   it runs
  it jumps!
   you reel
walk backwards
      reel
hit the drag!
   hit the drag!
you reel
  the early morning's
rays reveal
    jewel-leaved trees

that line the shore
   you reel
      he's got the net!
it's yours!
         finally—the first
            on the river
   in October
         with you

little bug

today i watched
a little bug
as it dug
a hole
five times its size
in the sand

back and forth
it ran
nonstop
content to dig
its tiny eyelash
legs grabbing
and pushing
the sand back
into a tidy
bug-size heap

efficient
silent
content
doing something
for the sake of
the cycle
the circle
of

its existence
with the countless
others of its kind
before

and
after
it

as i sit
and
wonder where
my ambition
went
plunder through
the guilt
of
idleness
the great kindness
of God's mercy
not lost
on
me

deep blue night

the faintest
  whitest of blues
the lonely, cold
  winter moon's hue
stands alone on black trees
 and the omniscient snow
whose show
  has beaten even
the stars

cars' tires creak
  as red-nosed drivers
 carefully creep
from one frosty spot
  to the next
and for a few hours
 the sun shows her face
to chase
away
the frozen
  air
of deep night
  a silent, complete
sight
    undisturbed
by foot
  or eye
as brave little bunnies
  go hopping by
and i search
 for my slippers

garden in a sandbox

the highwayman came riding
  into my melodramatic heart
 Rod McKuen took the hand
of my loneliness
     and gave it a name
  that didn't rhyme
out of time, i placed myself far
    from where i was,
     scribbled and cried my youth away
  swayed in a daze
to the songs
    that accompanied my uncles to Vietnam
and crash-landed my self-esteem
   into a dreamlike maze
    of make believe fate
it was too late when i realized
 i didn't want to be pushed
by someone who wanted to invent the buttons
(maybe that's unfair—
          maybe all he wanted was love)
  i'm not above sin,
   can't get around the plow
  that reins me now to where
    i've always been
as it breaks the ground of fields
  my soul hid from before
i didn't think a garden could grow in sand,
   so i bought a plantation
    where i pictured heaven
     and paid for it
       with my naiveté

              sold it to my tears
now
            i'm building castles
          in the same old sandbox
           i couldn't wait to leave
             finding it hard to believe
                the luck
             (hard but generous)
               at the chance
                to inherit my Childhood again,
                 and truly live while i'm alive,
                   among the places that i know
                    and those i love,
simple blessings from above
            more exotic
              than anywhere
         my two feet could carry me.

"For this cause I bow my knees unto the Father of our Lord Jesus Christ, Of whom the whole family in heaven and earth is named, That he would grant you, according to the riches of his glory, to be strengthened with might by his Spirit in the inner man; That Christ may dwell in your hearts by faith; that ye, being rooted and grounded in love, May be able to comprehend with all saints what is the breadth, and length, and depth, and height; And to know the love of Christ, which passeth knowledge, that ye might be filled with all the fullness of God. Now unto him that is able to do exceeding abundantly above all that we ask or think, according to the power that worketh in us, Unto him be glory in the church by Christ Jesus throughout all ages, world without end. Amen."

Ephesians 3:14-21 (KJV)

love

among the ashes

love unfolds the layers
   of its petals
      as
   somewhere inside i bloom
while on the surface
   my strength wilts away
      for it takes some pain
  to grow
   yet somehow
   i still don't know
why
   i will try
      not to ask that
to go back
   to a child's simultaneous wonder
and acceptance
   existence
        content
safe in Faith
   alive in Him

every man craves

Lord, your Love
   it never fails
Your majesty
    my wounds gently heals
as each day
   through your word
    and ways
You reveal the hope
the heart of
   every man craves,
and pour out
   Your grace,
the heart of every man
     to lovingly save.

deep fire of love

how long must i wait before
i lose
     my temper?
it's been so quick for so long
it's hard to slow it down
let alone
   let it go
and doing so
   allow myself
    to truly love

for patience is
as essential as trust
when it comes to real love

 lust
       hurries our
             hearts along
                        past the tired beats
               of slow songs
                      into trouble

but patience
 lets us clear the rubble
and reach the other survivors
   with sanity and integrity intact
    knowing love is more than
our childish desire
  to jump right in
    only to later wish
we could retract

sometimes you
can bring
a scarlet hue
to the heart of
my ire

but in the same instant
when it could be lost
i must remember the cost
of my temper
and weather the moment's rage
with a breath
that keeps the deeper
fire of love aflame

A Father's Love

Oh, Father, i can feel your love
   washing down over my soul
     every moment,
        every thought
    every heartbeat
      yours, Lord, yours
shaking at your Spirit's touch,
   awestruck, humbled
  by such overwhelming love
trust
    that comes by faith,
    living and looking toward
      that which is unseen,
hope our common denominator
You, Lord, our Father, Creator
i can feel your love come down,
   shimmering unseen showers
      of grace
   tears of shame
        that roll down my face
wiped away by
   your bittersweet sacrifice,
   by your love, your life
for mine freely given

smiling down from heaven,
   loving all your children
      despite their sins
glorified by the love we share
   in your name
Happy Father's Day, dear Lord.

above the clouds

a picture holds a thousand words, they say
  there's one, looking down through the clouds
    that takes me away
to a day
  when the sun was warm
               the sky was blue
and me and you
  climbed a mountain inside a
red T-top bird
    and our hearts spoke
  the secrets they had always heard
      each other whispering
trees and houses thread
  upon the patchwork hills
  that roll westward from doubt
    to home and loved ones
              and you
  the two of us held hands at the top,
stop inside the tower
    to look back down
        the road we've come
in one moment
  the whole day
    and now
        from somewhere
inside my joy returns
    and I'm a child again
when you tell me you love me
  as we stand
    hand in hand
        above the clouds

right out loud

Gramma,
even though
i know it won't change
what's history now
  i can't help but contemplate
the could have beens
  and try to change
my ways somehow
before it's too late again

i took it for granted,
  your being there
i did not recognize it then
  but as i stare
up this lonely road
  now i know what was
    and what could have been
      what should have been

i won't list them now,
    won't lament
  for not loving you more
  so you knew before you
went home
  that even though i'd grown
into a woman with my own life,
  i would always be
    your Crissy

how could i forget?
    i wear your face,
      just like your oldest

i pray now
  i am granted the Grace
to allow me
    to do your memory proud
and let my loved ones know
    i care
  right out loud

thank you for your prayers
for my loved ones

i know you prayed for me today
because i felt God's Love come down
surround
me
with His sheltering arms,
comfort me with His Grace

i know you prayed for me today
because i felt God's Forgiveness,
    His Mercy
    my inspiration
      to become what i can—
   to begin right now, today

to say
"here i am, Lord"
    and not be afraid

i know you prayed for me today
because i felt your Love come down
    as a feather from Heaven's crown,
 come softly to serenade my soul
whole
again

power of Your love

Lord, heal the hearts
   of Your people
      in this world
trace their paths
    in Your perfect ways
lift their hands together
    You to joyfully praise
Let us sing a song
    that glorifies Your name
  give our souls over
  to the power of Your love
let our wills be won
by only You, Lord
   the Highest, Most Exalted One!

"For I am convinced that nothing can ever separate us from His Love. Death can't, and life can't. The angels won't, and all the powers of hell itself cannot keep God's Love away. Our fears for today, our worries about tomorrow, or where we are—high above the sky, or in the deepest ocean—nothing will ever be able to separate us from the Love of God demonstrated by our Lord Jesus Christ when he died for us."

Romans 8:38-39 (NIV)

snowshoeing in flip-flops

the snow is high
    and ice shades
        the windows of my heart
as i start
    to let resentment
  g r o w
    into what i know
 is a monster
      once unleashed
so i've unsheathed
  my sword
that the Lord
    has blessed me with
to transform the pith
 into syrup
    for cold waffles,
my standstill to
a stiff shuffle,
ruffle the feathers of
    my chicken suit
loot my heart
    for the love
    my soul for the hope
    my eyes for the truth

Everything

what are we without you, Lord
but dust and shapeless shadows

where can we go without you, Lord
but nowhere at all

what can we reap
without you, Lord, to sow
the seeds that grow our souls

what call
is there to answer
unless there is your voice?

what choice
could we make
that would be better
than loving You?

who knows
the inside of our hearts
as You, our Maker, do?
surely not ourselves

who but You
would give everything
to keep our lowly souls
from the clutches of hell?

what can we do
without You, Lord?

nothing.

what are we, Lord
without You?

nothing.

what are You to
each one of us?

Everything.

why?
because You first
loved us.

loving

time alone with nature
   time alone with you
is exactly the refueling
    my soul needed
  the every day mundane
    to make it through

i'm learning how
   to love—or rather
  what love truly is—
and it's so much more
   than that
passionate midnight kiss

it's holding your hand
  as the sun goes down
and greeting you
   "all smiles"
    as it comes up again
it's you thinking of me,
  even when
   you could first
   think of yourself

it's losing myself
  in the moment with you
knowing
   of all life's many
     journeys and tasks,

loving is the most
important one,
and love in return
is more than i
could ask.

undeserving heir

i knew you as a child
   but as time passed i slipped away
until i became the distant wretch
   that kneels before you today
i always knew you were there
   to take away my pain
but i let my roadmap gather dust
   and i forgot my family name
i wandered down an aimless road
   wasted my days consumed in sin
i complained about my heavy load
   when a freeloader is what i've been
adulteress, liar, thief
   idle lover to shame and grief
doubting what i knew as true
i kept swimming away from you

until i thought i'd drowned

i know i don't deserve it,
i can hardly believe it,
but i can finally feel
the hand you've been reaching down
from your very throne
to pull me from my hell,
once again remove the shell
and reform my lifeless soul
your unending mercy and love
   the only drug i need to
     make me whole again

and when i feel the
    slimy seaweeds reaching up
    from the depths to pull me down
once more,
you throw me the strong rope of
    your grace
    and gently pull me ashore
to rest with you
   on the peaceful white sands
    of your love that will reign
forevermore.

faith

broken paradise

for His Glory
   He created Earth
the moon, the stars,
   the sun
and everything
      under it—
even man.

here we stand
   upon our broken paradise
wondering why
   He
     has forsaken us?

but what
   has man created
 to compare
     with water clear
   and pure air?

aren't our
   machines
a little worse
   for the wear
    without our constant care?

who upgrades the trees
   or redefines the
      mountains?
  that man who
   moved the stars,
  what was his name again?

when will we accept
   the story of our birth
   understand
   the meaning of our life
 and embrace our death
       that means to live again
        with Him?

there is a reason

if I can be strong enough to
      let go of my life
maybe I can walk into
         the true light
not true love
  or luck
  or true happiness,
     not success

just be   just let
   God guide
     and stop the guess -
- ing

never gets me very far
  except perhaps to fear
  true lies
   and lust
   true helplessness
     emptiness
          and when
i've been to Hell
on the bare back of
     my free will
    and stayed until i'm tan

His hand is outstretched
      patient,
  offering
     rescue

                        e
                    m

                d
               e
             h
            c
           t
         e
       r
to   w
even when i can't see
   His spirit in me
   finally finding true peace
when i see
   there is a reason
           for me
         larger than
        my own life

i can begin again

the devil's on attack
  but Jesus has my back
His Spirit will give me the power
  to devour my desires for sin
unfathomable gifts
   are mine as i begin
      to live again
  ashamed of what
   and where and who
     i've been
    but not forgotten
    or forsaken
for Jesus has taken my sins
   upon His cross
and with my Lord as my boss
  though i can't reach perfection
with His Spirit's intervention
 and his loving promise of Life
i can begin again
     each day
     each night
to change my ways
  and sing His praise
with a life lived for Him

make it Yours

take what is mine, Lord
and make it yours
make your Glory
and your pleasure
what I'm living for

take my worry,
take my guilt
take the best there is in me
take my shame
and my sins, Lord
let your Love
wash me clean

take my time, Lord
take my talents
take all you've given me
and let them all work
through me for your sake
take what is mine, Lord
and make it yours.

let me shine

let me shine
let my love
be the light
that burns a way
through hate and crime
let me shine
and rise above
the demons
that would stand
in my way
and steal my time

let me shine
and be a flame
that burns a path
for my enemies
to follow
let me shine
and speak your name
so that this hollow
world will learn
You are Lord

let me shine
let Your love
live in me
and lead the way
let me shine
and darkness hide
from the wonder
of the faith
you've given me

let me shine
let me grow
to know you more
let me shine
and show the world
it's You
i'm living for
let me shine

from my knees

words fall away
   as i fall to my knees
and praise You
   for all You've given us
please, Lord forgive me
  for my many sins
    for i know it's only You
       i can trust
from my knees, Lord
    let me conquer my fears,
let Your truth
     and Your way
      lead my life
for the things of this world
   they all pass away
      until all we can cling to
        is faith
please, Lord
   let your Spirit fill me
      today

daughter of the King

i considered myself an outcast,
   a black sheep,
      misunderstood
I lived my life by my own rules
   and i've been alone
      even in love
afraid, confused, even hopeless
   full of dreams
      but frozen and aimless
ashamed
   but now i'm blameless
  for i've called on Your name
and by the mysterious mercy
   of Your Love
 i've found that life isn't lived
until it's for You
   and through faith
i'm born again,
   no longer an outcast,
but a daughter of
      the King

mysteries too awesome

eternity, it scares me
   the thought of never an end
but then i also tremble
   to think of not being and death
no, my feeble mind can't grasp
   the concept of life everlasting
for here on this earth
   there comes an end to everything

neither can i comprehend You, Lord
   and your unconditional, merciful love
or why you would care for wretched me, Lord
   looking down from Your throne above
i've never seen Your Son face to face,
   never touched the holes in His hands
but i believe He's the only way, Lord
   and i know that You do love me
for i've seen Your works—
   all the earth and the sea—
and i've read Your word
   i've seen Your love reflected
in innocent babies' eyes
   and as i've walked life's difficult road,
Lord, i've felt Your hand in mine

the sun as it rises each morning,
   and the stars in the darkness shining
are miracles themselves to behold
   and Your Spirit living inside me
moves my soul and, Lord, i know
   You are real, the only One
and even at death, my life's just begun

so i'll leave to You the mysteries
   too awesome for my mind to hold
and live without fear of eternity,
   or worry about getting old
for Your grace that covers my sins, Lord
   can also cover my fears
and Your wisdom and mercy, O Lord
   are not measured in mere mortal years

Praise Jesus!
amen

rejoice!

rejoice! for God, He loves us
though unworthy we surely are
rejoice! for Jesus' blood has saved us,
washed us clean and healed our many scars

rejoice! the Holy One Most High,
King of Kings has a wonderful plan for you
rejoice! and wear a smile through that sorrow,
for the Lord, He will bring you through
and show you His glorious tomorrow
and reveal what He has for you to do!

rejoice! for God, He loves us all,
though unworthy we still remain
rejoice! for Jesus is coming again
to take us home with Him to heaven,
separated forever from pain!

ultimate defense

thank You, Lord
   for Your mercy,
     for Your sacrifice
for it wonderfully
   overwhelms me
     the wonder of Your love
   that You would
     give Your life
for the sake of mine

   Lord, the trap of time
     is that it never ends,
and our greatest joy
   is that You have
     our ultimate defense—
to save us from
   our death in sin,
You came to earth
   and walk with men

bright inside

bring me out of hiding, Lord
   bring my heart back to itself
please forgive me for
   the days i've wasted
help me make the most
   of those i've left
help me love, Lord
   like You do
help me model myself
   after You
let Your light shine
       bright inside
so that my soul
          no longer hides

to my knees

as the morning sun
    kisses the eyelids
        of the dewy green earth
and my two sound eyes
        take it in
and the birds their fragile praises sing
to my two ears
      like a hymn
    this morning
       awakens for you,
in your grace in all we do
    unable to perceive
    all the wonders of
    the result of your love
    without falling
        to my knees—
o, Lord, let me begin and end each day
    that way
    and when i speak,
        let me say,
          You reign.

            Amen

He is in control

this must be why
    they call it a fight—
it's not til you lose a few battles
  you realize that.

faith is revealed, too
   when you
      begin to understand
  God is still willing
  and as His child
  you cannot lose
     as long as you remember
  He is in control

catch a fish or two

carry yourself lightly
    throw away your pride
   recycle what you've learned
spend some quality time
       with the Almighty
in the home He made for you
catch a fish or two
    save a soul if you can
remember to think of your
                self
last
    carry forward from the past
only that which glorifies God,
    ever trusting in
       our Lord Jesus Christ
forgive yourself and others
    and do what you know is right
    even when the burden
     is far from light,
   knowing hope lies
     in our Lord
and meeting Him in heaven
    will soon be our reward.

    Praise Jesus!

Peace in Your Grace

Heavenly Father, up above
let me give You my worries
to wash away with Your Love

let me find Peace in Your Grace
and confess my sins
with an uplifted face

humble stature

tell me about
    the Good News,
preacher,
    tell me all about
    who Jesus is
so that in my heart
    His Spirit lives
and His Word
        comes alive
  in my mind
for evil finds
    a home
in too many places
    today
  in so many ways
we need you, o Lord
    and from our
    humble stature
we praise
    your holy name!

worthy

what can i say to You,
    oh, God?
for You know all things,
   even my unspoken thoughts
what could i say
   that would be worthy
     of You?
of works, great or small,
   which is worthy of You?
nothing, oh, Lord, can
i say or do
   that would ever come close
     to being worthy of You
the awe of Your majesty
confounds my mind
   until the only words
   i can find
   are "i believe."
   thank You, Lord,
that You found us worthy
of dying for.

hope

He continues to bless me
with His love, grace and peace
but still there are times
when i feel ill at ease

for a sinner i am
and try as i can,
far from perfect
i will always be

so i live
and i love
and i converse with Above
Friend to friend

and i hope in the end
i'll begin

Lord, open their hearts

Lord, i pray for our loved ones
who don't know your name
or the wonderful, awesome
forgiveness that came
when in your boundless love
you sent your only son
to walk among
lowly sinners
such as us

in your eternal wisdom
saw him hung
on the cross of our shame
so that by his sacrifice
you could call us each by name
to come home at last
to the grace you afford
through the blood of
the only holy one,
Christ Jesus, our Lord

Lord, i pray that by your grace
and great love
you would send your Spirit
down from above
to open the ears
of their hearts so they'd hear
your knocking at the door of their soul,
ever and always, so near
to their every thought, every need
ever their only hope, indeed
Lord, please open their minds
to your mysteries

fill your children with your light
so that we may be
bright pillars of your love
in this dark and scary place
forever bold, yet gentle
encouraging others toward your grace

let your love shower down, Lord
and wash all our sins away
let them hear your majestic voice
as again and again you say
"come, and follow me,
the truth, the only way
I have so much love for you
if only you'd open your heart
and let me stay."

Lord, i lift up our unsaved loved ones
i ask you to call their names
and let them hear you and come running
to follow you all their days

amen

a prayer for the new year

let me not grow stagnant, Lord
but let me truly
live each day
let me not lament
my sinfulness,
but help me, Lord
rejoice in Your ways
let me love
like you would
have me to, my King
let me in everything
first look to You
let your love
be my light
let your Spirit take flight
on the wings of
your peoples' faith
let me remember You
first, always

in God's hands

God's word is alive
—it took me by the hand today
and led me
from my sin and shame
to the place
where my Lord and King
gently takes my hand
and helps me stand
tall and strong
as His child
the river wild
of my mind
tamed only
by His kind ways
and loving words,
the tapestry of
my life
a masterpiece
only when
left in His hands
and so i stand,
a child of God

until it overflows

i need you, Lord
to light the way,
just to make it
through today

to let your Grace,
your Love, your Truth
wash over everything
i say and do

for i am desperate
if without you
and there would be
no hope

but for the rope
of rescue
You throw
to each of us
every day—

the bridge that
closes the gap
completely,
lifts us up
and lets us be
confident
in Your love,
the greatest gift
which no man
could give—

the cross
where your Son
paid the cost
of all our sins

and so your love
which never ends
begins again
anew each day,

our everlasting,
one true friend
You hold our hands
even when

no one but You
could love us

and so i trust
in the only one i can
i look to you, Lord
to take my hand
again
today
and make your way
come to life
within my soul
until it overflows
and the whole world
knows of
your love.

Jesus on my side
(a song)

devil, get behind me
cuz God is on my side
He's set Jesus here
before me
to always be my guide
and with his arms around me
there's no way
you can get through,
cuz with Jesus
right beside me,
i'm already a step ahead of you

already a step ahead of you
with Jesus by my side
so, devil get behind me,
i don't have time
to hear your lies
i've got Jesus now
to save me,
He's opened up my eyes,
so, devil get behind me,
i've got Lord Jesus
on my side.

"I press on toward the goal to win the prize for which God has called me heavenward in Christ Jesus."

Phillipians 3:14 (NIV)

"Now the God of peace, that brought again from the dead our Lord Jesus, that great shepherd of the sheep, through the blood of the eternal covenant, Make you perfect in every good work to do his will, working in you that which is wellpleasing in his sight, through Jesus Christ; to whom be the glory for ever and ever. Amen."

> Hebrews 13:20-21 (KJV)

Printed in the United States
80432LV00006B/52-114